Paver Projects

Designs for Amazing Outdoor Environments

Melissa Cardona
PaverModule

Schiffer Publishing Ltd
4880 Lower Valley Road, Atglen, PA 19310 USA

Acknowledgments

This beautiful book would not have possible without the amazing photographic talent of the Greg Wilson Group and W.F. Jennings. Many thanks to them for their creative vision, demonstrating the beauty and versatility of concrete pavers. Also, thanks to all the installation craftsmen, design professionals, and employees of PaverModule, whose hard work, dedication, and creativity appear on the following pages.

Greg Wilson Group
Architectural & Commercial Photography
Sarasota, FL
www.gregwilsonphoto.com

W.F. Jennings
Hollywood, FL

Library of Congress Control Number: 2005931494

Designed by "Sue"
Type set in Bedrock/Zurich LtCn BT

ISBN: 0-7643-2345-8
Printed in China

Published by Schiffer Publishing Ltd.
4880 Lower Valley Road
Atglen, PA 19310
Phone: (610) 593-1777; Fax: (610) 593-2002
E-mail: Info@schifferbooks.com

For the largest selection of fine reference books on this and related subjects, please visit our web site at www.schifferbooks.com

We are always looking for people to write books on new and related subjects. If you have an idea for a book please contact us at the above address.

This book may be purchased from the publisher.
Include $3.95 for shipping.
Please try your bookstore first.
You may write for a free catalog.

In Europe, Schiffer books are distributed by
Bushwood Books
6 Marksbury Ave.
Kew Gardens
Surrey TW9 4JF England
Phone: 44 (0) 20 8392-8585; Fax: 44 (0) 20 8392-9876
E-mail: info@bushwoodbooks.co.uk
Free postage in the U.K., Europe; air mail at cost.

Contents

Introduction

This portfolio of paver projects showcases hundreds of real-life installations of concrete pavers. It is meant to inspire designers, landscape professionals, and architects by illustrating the virtually limitless potential of pavers to create attractive and durable outdoor environments. With enough creativity and imagination, almost anything is possible. Some of the paver styles or colors featured here are not in PaverModule's product literature because they have been manufactured to fit custom specifications developed by customers who want to achieve a special look for their projects. And the hope is that you, too, will see something to spark your imagination and create a wonderful, unique design.

Versatility, strength, and availability make pavers an ideal choice for all projects. From residential to commercial and municipal applications, concrete pavers outperform other paving materials, while adding lasting beauty. This portfolio showcases a huge variety of projects and styles, including classic, contemporary, Mediterranean, Old World, elegant, and playful designs. While a project's setting may dictate the style and pattern of pavers you choose, the dynamic goes both ways, with pavers having the ability to help establish the personality of the place where they reside.

This book has been broken up into Residential and Commercial and Public Projects, and then within those sections, into chapters featuring different components of paver projects—paths, patios, roads, entrances, and more are all included to help catalyze ideas for your own projects. Styles and patterns can be interchanged—just because a certain pattern appears in a hotel patio doesn't mean it can't be used in someone's backyard. Similarly, a design featured in the residential section can be translated and applied to any commercial or municipal project. Your only limit is creativity and imagination, and we hope that this amazing portfolio of paver projects opens the door to an unending fount of ideas.

Residential Projects

Driveways

Brick-shaped pavers arranged in a parquet or herringbone pattern provide a simple, classic look that complements any home's style. Different effects can be created with different looks. Pavers with rounded edges, like those in the project below, give the appearance of age, while the standard pavers lend themselves to a more contemporary look.

Attractive effects can also be achieved by using different colored pavers within the same application. Here, the gated drive leads to the garage and around the home's showpiece entrance, where pavers in multiple colors really draw attention and create a suitable stage from which such a grand home should rise.

Pavers complement any architectural style. From traditional to contemporary, or small and casual to formal and grand, the possibilities of paver projects are limitless—especially with the huge variety of colors, shapes, and textures available.*

These pavers complement the look of a Spanish Mission Revival Style home and add a dimension of age to the newly constructed property.

TOP: The pavers in these driveways were chosen to match the hue of the homes' tiled roofs.
BOTTOM: Paver colors can match the home's existing color scheme, or add a contrasting hue for interest. These projects feature relatively neutral tones that were chosen to blend into the home's palette.

Pavers in mixed and matched dark tones attractively pair with the dark trim of Tudor-inspired architecture.

These large pavers give the driveway a plaza-like personality.

The hue of a home brings out the subtle colors and textures of the driveway's pavers.

A herringbone patterned paver driveway lends a refined look to the formal entrance of this home.

Tumbled pavers were chosen for the driveway of this mid-century designed home, creating a dynamic contrast of historical and modern styles.

Pavers define the sweeping entrance and driveway into a grand home with a gated entrance to the garage and more private areas of the property.

Large stones mark the border of a paver driveway and provide an effective drainage area during heavy rains.

Contrasting paver colors and shapes were used for these driveways' borders to add drama.

Here, pavers in a border were also used continuously along paths running within the driveway's edges.

In this driveway, contrasting pavers create an elegant grid pattern that matches the grand, Old World Style architecture of the home.

Lines of dark colored pavers border and intersect this driveway to create interest, which is also garnered with the placement of a decorative circle in front of the home's sprawling entrance. Notice the way freeform paver platforms seem to spill forth from the front door.

Pavers in nontraditional shapes can create patterns that serve as focal points—adding sophistication and interest to a home's hardscaping.

This paver pattern takes on a very different effect when the central block is included in white.

Pavers in contrasting textures were used to create this pattern. The design featuring the more vividly colored pavers has a stronger impact.

Patterns can be planned and repetitive or more random, depending on the look you wish to achieve.

Centerpieces + Focal Points

Traditional brick-shaped pavers were placed in a circular pattern radiating around the driveway's central landscaped island.

A driveway must be in proportion with the home's scale. Here, a landscaped island was added to maintain a residential feeling, scaling down the driveway's perceived size with a green and blooming focal point.

A small fountain was installed in the center of this home's driveway—a refined centerpiece to complement grand architecture.

This driveway looks like it should lead to a ballroom, not a garage. Nonetheless, design-conscious doors and living topiary create a focal point worthy of a royal palace, while this home makes an elegant statement to the street.

This driveway features a simple square to mark a focal point just outside the garage doors.

Here, a circle of dark pavers marks the center of and brings a sense of order to the vast expanse of this grand home's driveway.

A home that combines Mediterranean and classical design elements features a driveway reminiscent of a Roman or Spanish plaza. The symmetrical design breaks up the vast expanse of space, while complementing the grand style of the home's architecture.

A less ornate pattern of squares was used to draw attention to the space outside of this garage. The pavers used in this driveway were manufactured to fit together with large joints for a distinctive appearance.

A seemingly plain driveway erupts into a colorful sunburst pattern, creating a stunning front yard plaza.

Attractive pavers cut a path across the front yard, circling around a spectacular sculpture.

Entrances

These driveways continue unbroken into their adjacent homes' main entrances, and even beyond.

These homeowners wanted to leave space for landscaping directly against the walls of their homes, breaking up the expanse of driveway pavers with lush foliage.

As seen before, this home's entrance path is demarcated by pavers laid in a contrasting pattern, but the same exact color palette as the rest of the drive. The floor of the front porch maintains the same hues, but was laid in yet another distinct pattern.

Pavers end at the edge of steps that lead to this home's entrance, which is covered in terracotta and Spanish decorative tiles.

Tumbled pavers lead the way directly into the house to make a lasting first impression that begins curbside.

Exterior décor elements placed symmetrically create quite an impression on this home's visitors.

A small landscaped area was used to break up the large expanse of this driveway's pavers and create a separate walkway leading up to the home's front door.

Curved platforms of pavers bordered in coping lead to the entrance of the home, which surprises visitors with an attractive decorative sunburst just outside the front door.

Paths + Walkways

LEFT and RIGHT: Tumbled pavers provide the perfect look for the walkway of this Mediterranean-style home. A landscaped island marks the intersection of two pathways, directing the flow of traffic and catching the eye of curbside onlookers.

A more formal walkway was installed from the street to the home's entrance, while a more casual looking footpath was chosen to connect the driveway with the front door.

ABOVE and LEFT: A portico covers a paver-made path from driveway into courtyard, with an entrance guarded by a beautiful iron gate.

This paver path takes on a more ornate appearance, with a carefully plotted pattern leading the way to this home's main entrance.

The paths that lead to these front doors are merely extensions of adjacent driveways.

A random patterned paver driveway narrows to create a meandering walkway to the home's entrance.

A contrasting border along a path's edges catches the eye, whereas a non-bordered path lets other design elements in the yard be focal points.

Pool Decks + Patios

A fountain forms a stunning centerpiece on this elegant patio. The use of landscaping helps to balance the ensemble of pool, fountain, and the rest of the patio.

Crystal blue pools glitter like jewels in stunning paver patio settings.

Landscaping plays a key role in the design of these pool-skirting patios. Plants and trees add décor to patios, providing a sense of security as well.

A narrow patio backs out onto Lake Las Vegas and provides a wonderful warm-weather setting. Pavers were used not only for the patio floor, but to create areas for landscaping as well.

A trellis supported by neoclassical columns sports a vine that blossoms in late summer, and is just the right choice for a patio made from tumbled pavers.

Depending on the look that is sought, simple or complex paver patterns work equally well, and attractively, on patios.

Interlocking concrete pavers are the flooring of choice for these gorgeous Floridian lanais.

Traditional and shell pavers were laid in the same pattern on two different patios to give distinct looks.

Narrow, brick-shaped pavers help this patio achieve a stately look.

Beautiful billows of red and pink blossoms complement the ruddy hues of this paver patio.

Pavers act like carpet on the floor of this impressive outdoor living space. To save money and add interest, the patio was designed to be surrounded by desert landscaping, rather then occupy the entire backyard.

There are many choices and design possibilities for coping that help define a pool's border and entry.

These homeowners opted for a fountain in their patio. Besides offering an attractive focal point, its soft murmur of water provides a soothing atmosphere.

A retaining wall holds back a small patch of grassy lawn to make way for this classic looking shell paver patio.

Sunsets are not the only eye-catching views on the patio, which is a stunning site to be savored in and of itself.

Commercial and Public Projects

Large Scale Pool Decks + Patios

This desert oasis features a variety of paver shapes and designs that designate separate areas within the large, public space. Proportion is an important consideration when choosing paver patterns, illustrated beautifully by this project. A fan-shaped pattern occupies the smaller patio area, while the larger, pool-skirting area includes a simple grid pattern.

NO DIVING

Red-tinted pavers contrast beautifully with the crystal blue water of these community and commercial pools.

This equally impressive pool was dressed in shell pavers, giving the impression of a beach-like location.

A brick-shaped paver patio surrounds an awe-inspiring hotel pool with multiple manmade cascades and rock formations.

Shell pavers were also used in this hotel's pool patio—but in two hues to create a simple, yet elegant pattern.

Pavers with a slight color variation were used to create a subtle pattern for this hotel pool's patio. A sleeker, more formal pattern was chosen for the covered walkways directly adjacent to the hotel.

Pavers in contrasting colors, textures, and shapes help to create interest in this sprawling resort pool patio. Shell and non-shell pavers make an especially attractive combination.

Grids and squares are popular motifs for large-scale patios, breaking up large expanses of space without being too busy.

Colored accent pavers make this grid pattern a little more ornate. The blue pavers complement the clubhouse's color scheme and add a playful nature to the design.

Landscaping was incorporated into the pattern created by this patio's pavers. At the far end of the patio, a recreational chessboard breaks up the large space and creates interest.

A landing above the pool area features this intersection, using the same pavers used below on the pool patio.

Curves dominate in this pool-skirting patio. Pavers were placed to follow the pool's outline, then contrasted with the more rigid, yet eye-catching grid pattern of square and brick-shaped pavers. To create a sense of continuity, the waving paver pattern was applied to pathways adjacent to the building.

A decorative pattern created with shell and non-shell pavers was used at one end of this pool as a focal point. Contrasting borders and lines highlight and add interest to a simpler pattern along the pool's other edges.

This exciting paver pattern creates energy on a commercial patio, mirroring the movement of passing clouds. A glass aggregate used in the paver manufacturing process provides a wonderful texture to the surface.

A waterfront patio at the Boca Hotel in Boca Raton, Florida, boasts an attractive motif made with tumbled brick-shaped shell pavers. Circles designate focal points and design cues for furniture placement. The same pavers used to create the motif were used for steps.

What material but pavers could do justice to such a commanding entrance? Pavers were used not only for public pathways, but also for this establishment's public drive. While multiple colors of pavers give order to the expansive space, white pavers give visual cues to drivers.

RESEARCH, AND INFORMATION TECHNOLOGY CENTER

Sweeping lines define the curved entrance of Nova University's library. The pattern created by light-colored pavers complements the structure's curved façade, while large and small square-shaped pavers create a pattern that suggests movement.

Pavers were used extensively in this large-scale commercial project. At the Westin Diplomat Hotel in Hollywood, Florida, interlocking concrete pavers create the surface of the hotel's front driveway and walkways. To keep a sense of continuity, pavers were even used to create a pedestrian crossing into the hotel's property from the main boulevard.

At the Miami International Airport, brightly colored pavers in a design reminiscent of ocean waves greet cars as they arrive to and exit the parking lot—indicative of the typical Miami experience. Pavers can help establish the nature of a certain location, or they can reflect and enhance the personality of a place.

A shopping center in Weston, Florida, was designed to resemble a traditional town center. Pavers used throughout the application create a sense of continuity and community. The center's sidewalks, roads, and driveways were all constructed using pavers for a coherent, beautiful look.

A variety of paver styles, patterns, and colors maintain a consistent look throughout the center, adding interest throughout while sending visual cues to pedestrians and drivers.

These pavers perform aesthetic as well as utilitarian functions.

A movies theater's entrance dazzles with a stunning compass rose design, creating a courtyard setting where moviegoers linger long after the final credits roll. Just outside the box office, pavers create an attractive, but plainer entrance meant strictly to host efficient business transactions.

A herringbone pattern bordered by shell pavers creates an exquisite entrance. Tumbled brick-shaped pavers in a variety of hues complement the color of the adjacent building.

Pavers lead country club members to the clubhouse in style. Tumbled pavers were chosen to complement the building's Old World look.

The road that leads into a gated community features pavers manufactured to look like aged cobblestone. The choice makes a lasting impression while complementing the development's Mediterranean style architecture.

Tumbled pavers and striking Spanish architectural elements make a formidable impression on guests who visit this gated community.

The entrance into an exclusive social club is characterized by cobble block pavers defined by a crisscrossing pattern.

Colored pavers attract pedestrians to an urban grocery store, where the pattern is continued in the atrium and mirrored in the far wall's motif.

The driveway leading up to this hotel was paved in a fan pattern for its aesthetic value, as well as to signal to drivers that they should slow down.

Square-shaped pavers in a complementary color scheme lead hotel guests from vehicles into the hotel lobby in style.

OMNI RESORT

At this resort, distinct paver styles were also used to distinguish between vehicular and pedestrian traffic areas. The brick-shaped pavers used for the driveway have a much more utilitarian aesthetic, but are dressed up with a grid of white pavers.

This modest drive and entrance are distinguished by the paver pattern's change in orientation.

A random pattern of pavers gives a classic look to this commercial building's walkway and entrance.

Similarly shaped pavers in a brick color were manufactured to give them an historic appearance. Terracotta tiles the entrance of the apartment rental office featured in this photograph, complementing the Mediterranean style of the building's architecture.

A drive made from pavers is more appropriate than asphalt in the Floridian landscape. In addition, the pavers provide a more distinguished look to this resort hotel.

Multiple pavers and patterns were chosen for the distinct areas of this hotel entrance. The variety of styles lends a dynamic and vibrant appearance to the space.

A parking lot paved in asphalt features special decorative areas constructed with pavers. Besides adding interest, these areas indicate to drivers that pedestrians may be passing through.

ONE WAY

These projects illustrate other ways in which pavers, as well as other methods like landscaping and planters can give visual cues about pedestrian crossing and traffic merging areas.

Here, octagon-shaped pavers create a parking area. An octagon-shaped motif constructed from white square-shaped pavers indicates that this is an area of little movement.

Here are some other examples of how pavers can be arranged to communicate an area where traffic moves more slowly.

So many roads, and so many paver styles and patterns used to create them.

Pavers can be used in small projects and large ones—like this community entrance, driveway, and parking area. Pavers are not only more attractive than asphalt, but cooler during the hot Floridian summers.

Brilliant, colorful pavers were used to create traditional tribal patterns on the median strip of a road running through an Indian reservation, catching the eye of drivers as they pass through to their final destinations.

Paths, Promenades, + Plazas

Straight as arrows, these paths provide direct routes to destinations in the distance.

A clock tower provides multiple options for crossing its threshold—a path for every mood.

Tumbled pavers provide the look of a path worn by centuries of footsteps.

A solitary bench in the distance is the only permanent company to this guarded footpath.

A border at the edge of the patio blocks off paths leading away, but directs passersby into a quaint gazebo.

Dark pavers line the edges of this path.

Eye-catching patterns attract the wanderer, leading them down paths where they never expected to go.

Distinct paver patterns direct the flow of pedestrian traffic, and make people slow down at the intersection of paths.

The same pavers used in the body of this path were oriented differently to create a border at its edges, and then lined with white shell pavers to create interest.

The undulating lines of this resort's oceanside walkways are an invitation to stroll leisurely; to take one's time and enjoy the ocean view. At the entrance of the building, the waving lines create movement and keep traffic flowing, especially during checkout.

Paths can wander up steps, or through a covered corridor. Paths can be plain, or patterned. With pavers, paths can be whatever you want them to be.

Converging paths cross, and continue around an island of green.

Whether paving the way to interior or exterior entrances, pavers offer many attractive options and looks depending on your needs.

A narrow waterfront walkway cuts an elegant path around the imposing architecture of this structure.

A waterfront promenade in Historic Malory Square in Key West, Florida, features a grid pattern within its borders to add interest and create movement.

Zigzagging black lines add energy to the paths of the Hard Rock Hotel and Casino in Hollywood, Florida.

This striking pattern of pavers travels the length of the beach—a colorful boardwalk that attracts all kinds of visitors to the shore.

The elegant landing of a private marina features concrete pavers laid in segments to fit the area's curved shape.

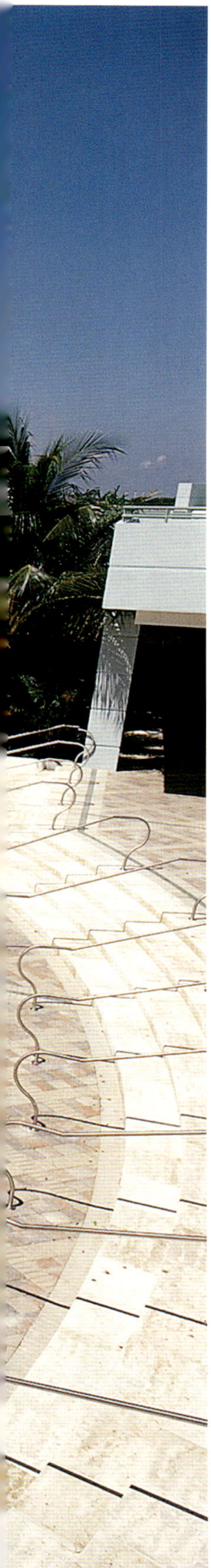

This hotel's enormous plaza is brought to a more human scale with the use of a grid pattern in pavers.

Outside a condominium, a beachfront promenade features square motifs that designate the area as one for gathering.

A shopping center plaza features distinct paver patterns to distinguish between separate areas with different uses.

Colorful pavers with glass aggregate and dynamic patterns add energy and momentum to the Hard Rock Hotel and Casino—where visitors come back time and time again for excitement, good times, and a memorable setting.

At Domino Park, in Miami, Florida, a bright and playful design draws the attention of passersby and helps to establish the park's identity with custom-designed domino tiles.

A more classic look was desired for this commercial center. Interior and exterior outdoor areas feature distinct paver patterns in complementary color schemes.

Because of its attractive plaza, this popular shopping destination in St. Petersburg, Florida, serves as more than just a commercial center, offering the community a place to gather publicly and enjoy the beautiful weather.

POP

Fountains serve as popular plaza centerpieces, with compass roses and stars as attractive adornments that visually bring it all together.

Though not a plaza, this cul-de-sac's fountain ensemble could easily be translated into a more pedestrian-friendly design.

This paver pattern seen in an earlier photograph of a commercial patio was used in other areas of the same shopping center. Here, a colorful and playful pattern surrounds the edge of a fountain to maintain the whimsical quality of the location.

PLAZA
SEMINOLE
IMPROV
SEMINOLE
INDIAN
VILLAGE
MUSEUM

The fan-shaped pattern of pavers complements the fountain's sculptural elements.

Red flowers punctuate the perimeter of this intersection's centerpiece for a dramatic effect among the stunning backdrop of a fan-shaped paver pattern.

Some more examples of fountains set within paver-laid plazas.

A neoclassical design approach combines with a tropical climate for a regal resort experience.

This neighborhood cul-de-sac is the envy of its residents' friends. Accent lines divide the circle of pavers and draw the eye towards a splashing fountain.

Elliptical lines of pavers encircle this fountain, the focal point of a shopping center plaza.

Circles overlap and splay out to encompass a landscaped island. A band of pink flowers wraps like a necklace around the base of the tree.

All paths eventually intersect, so why not do it in style. Here, pavers wrap around the base of this landscaped island for an attractive statement.

A median strip surrounded in pavers is punctuated by a profusion of lush, tropical landscaping.

Miami's Torch of Friendship memorial is characterized by an artistic and seemingly freeform design, which continues along the adjacent boulevard's sidewalks. The effect creates excitement and mimics the movement of cars on the road.

Paths circling two municipal ballparks converge at a three-dimensional baseball designed with pavers. Rather than just laying flat, the design domes above the rest of the walkways in order to be more of a focal point.